New Testament

Good News for Mary 96

Old and New Kings 104

Jesus Helps a Little Girl 108

The Boy Who Gave Jesus His Lunch 120

The Searching Shepherd 132

The Loving Father 148

The Stranger Who Cared 164

A Farmer Sows Seeds 181

Two Builders – Two Houses 195

Jesus the King 208

Jesus Lives! 217

My Toddler Bible

Published by Candle Books
an imprint of
Lion Hudson plc
Wilkinson House, Jordan Hill Road,
Oxford OX2 8DR, England
www.lionhudson.com/candle

ISBN 978 1 78128 241 0

First edition 2016

A catalogue record for this book is available
from the British Library

Printed and bound in China, January 2016, LH06

My Toddler
Bible

by Juliet David
illustrated by Chris Embleton-Hall

CANDLE
BOOKS

Old Testament

In the Beginning 8

A Wonderful Garden 16

Noah and His Great Ark 24

Abraham Moves Home 32

Joseph and His Brothers 40

The Baby in the Basket 50

David and the Giant Bully 58

Daniel and the Lions 71

Jonah Gets the Message 82

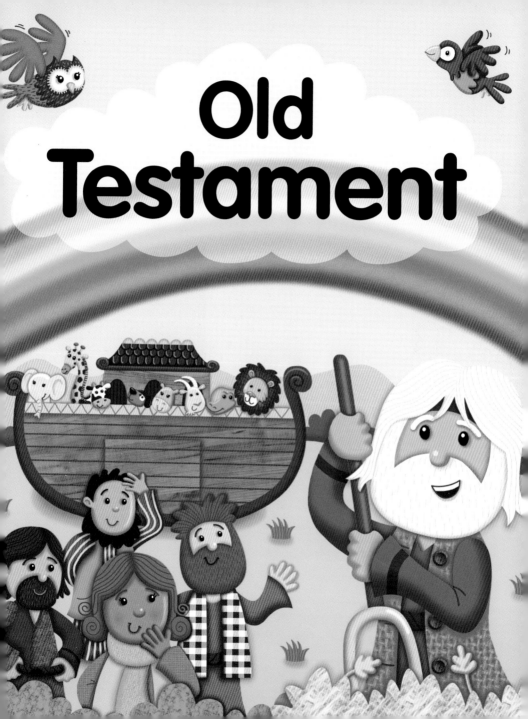

Old Testament

In the Beginning

At the beginning God made heaven and earth.
But everything was very dark and empty.

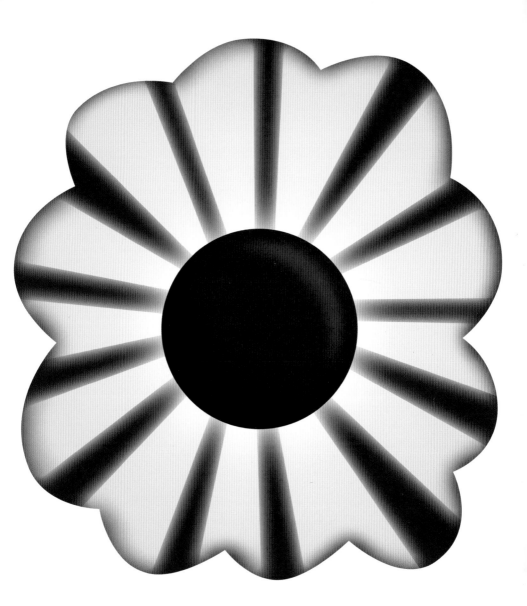

So God said, "Let there be light!"
And there was light.

The next day, God filled the sea with water.
Then he put air and clouds in the sky.
"It's all good!" said God.

On the third day, God made the land.
He created hills and valleys.
Then he filled the land with trees and flowers.

On day four, God placed the sun in the sky.
Night was dark, so he put the
moon and stars in the sky.

On the fifth day, God filled the sea with fish and
everything that swims. He filled the sky with birds.
"It's all good!" said God.

On day six, God made all the animals. Lions and tigers, cats and dogs, giraffes and hippos. Then God made the first man, Adam. And the first woman, Eve.

The seventh day dawned. God was tired
after all this making, so he rested.
Everything he had made was very good!

A Wonderful Garden

God gave Adam and Eve a beautiful garden called Eden. They lived there so happily with the animals.

But God gave them a warning.
"Never, *ever*, eat the fruit of this tree!" he said.

One day a sneaky snake slithered up to Eve.
"Go on, eat some fruit from *this* tree," he whispered.

So Eve took a bite.
She disobeyed God.

Along came Adam.
"Here, eat some!" said Eve, offering him the fruit.
And he did.

That afternoon God came to find them.
"Why are you both hiding from me?" he asked.
"We ate some of *that* fruit," said Adam.

"Then you must leave the garden," said God.
So Adam and Eve were sent out of the garden.

Now they had to work hard, growing food.
Digging and sowing, weeding and watering.
Hard, tiring work! *So* different from life in Eden.

Noah and His Great Ark

"A great flood is coming!" God warned Noah.
"You must build a great ark to hold you,
your family, and two of every sort of animal."
So Noah and his sons built a huge boat.

Soon it was finished.
Now they gathered two of every sort of animal.
They led them all into the ark.
Dark clouds started to appear. Soon it would rain.

The storm began. Rain fell and the water rose.
Before long the ark was afloat on the water.
But Noah, his family, and the animals
were all safe on board the ark.

Inside the ark, Noah and his sons
had stored plenty of food for the animals.
Every day they fed the animals
and gave them water to drink.

At last, after forty days and nights, the rain stopped.
Slowly, slowly the water went down.
Then, with a mighty bump,
the ark landed on a mountain.

Noah sent out a dove to find out if it was safe
for everyone to leave the ark.
Soon she returned carrying an olive leaf.
There was dry land again!

Noah opened the great door of the ark.
Out streamed all the animals.
Out flew all the birds.
How happy they were to be free again!

God put a wonderful rainbow in the sky.
"*Never again* will I flood the whole earth,"
God promised. "Every time you see the rainbow,
remember my words."

Abraham Moves Home

Abraham and Sarah lived in a far-off land.
One day God said to Abraham,
"I am going to take you to a new land."

So Abraham and Sarah set out on a long journey.
They took with them their camels, their cattle,
and their sheep and goats.
God showed them the way to go.

After many months, they arrived.
"*This* is the land I promised you," said God.
Abraham and Sarah were very happy
in this new land.

Sarah was very old – but she had no children.
One dark night God promised Abraham,
"In time there will be as many people in your family
as there are stars in the sky."

Soon after, three visitors came to Abraham's tent. "Please have lunch with me," he said.

After the meal, one of the visitors said to Abraham,
"Next year Sarah will have a baby!"

Sarah was listening through the tent wall.
She laughed!
"There's *no way* I can have a baby at my age!"

But sure enough, a year later Sarah had a baby boy.
She named him "Isaac".
God kept his promise to Abraham and Sarah.

Joseph and His Brothers

Old Jacob had twelve sons. He loved them all.
But Jacob loved his young son Joseph
more than *all* the rest.

One day Jacob gave Joseph a very special coat.
His brothers felt jealous.
Why did Joseph *always* get the best presents?

One day Jacob told Joseph,
"Your brothers are away minding my sheep.
Take some food to them."
So Joseph set off to find his brothers.

But when he arrrived, Joseph's cruel brothers sold him to traders, who carried him off to Egypt. There they sold him to a rich man called Potiphar.

Joseph worked hard for Potiphar.
But Potiphar's wife told him some lies about Joseph.
Poor Joseph was quickly flung into prison!

The king of Egypt's servant was also in prison.
One night he had a strange dream.
"Your dream means the king wants you to
work for him again," explained Joseph.
Sure enough, the servant soon left jail.

Some time later, the king also had a strange dream.
Seven fat cows came out of the river –
then seven skinny cows swallowed the fat cows.
No one knew what it meant!
Suddenly the king's servant remembered Joseph.

"Bring Joseph here!" ordered the king.
"Your dream means God will send seven good
harvests – then seven years with no harvest,"
explained Joseph. "Store up grain in the good years –
then everyone can eat in the bad years."

"I want *you* to be in charge of storing the grain,"
said the king. "You're very clever."
So, when the hungry years came, Joseph
made sure everyone had enough to eat.

When the food ran out, old Jacob
sent his sons to Egypt to buy grain.
Joseph wept for joy to see his brothers again.
Now they felt *very* sorry they had sold him.

The Baby in the Basket

One day the cruel king of Egypt gave a terrible order.
"Throw *every* Israelite baby boy into the river!"

One Israelite mother hid her baby in the house.
But she was afraid a soldier might hear him crying.
So she made a basket from reeds.

When it was finished, she went to the river
and floated her baby in the basket.
"Hide here and watch!"
she told her daughter, Miriam.

The princess came to bathe.
She soon noticed the basket.
"What a beautiful baby!" gasped the princess.
"How I wish he were mine!"

Miriam crept up. "Do you need a nurse
for the baby?" she asked.
"Yes please!" said the princess.
So Miriam ran home to fetch her mother.

"This woman could look after the baby,"
said Miriam, pointing to her mother.
"Look after him well!" said the princess.
"When he's old enough, bring him to live with me."

A few years later, the boy's mother
took him to the king's palace.
"I will name him 'Moses'!" said the princess.

So Moses was brought up
as a prince in the palace.
But Moses never forgot that God saved him
from the cruel king of Egypt.

David and the Giant Bully

David was a young shepherd boy.
He had lots of older brothers.

One day David set out to visit his brothers.
They were fighting for God's people.
His mother gave him food to take to them.

When David arrived at the army camp,
he discovered everyone was terrified.

The enemy had a giant called Goliath on their side.
"Who dares to fight me?" he yelled.
Nobody answered!

David went to find the king.
"I will fight this terrible giant for you," David offered.

But everyone just laughed!

"All right," said the king.
"Though I don't think you'll beat him."
His men laughed again.

"I'll lend you my sword and my helmet," said the king. But they were *much* too big for young David.

So David went out to fight the huge giant.
He had no sword and no shield.
He just had his shepherd's sling.
David chose five smooth little stones from the stream.

"Just a few little stones?" growled the giant.
"You don't scare me!"

David slung his first stone.
Wheeee! It whizzed through the air.
The little stone hit Goliath right on his forehead.

Crrrrashhh! Thummpp!
The giant dropped to the ground.
All the enemy soldiers ran away.
God helped young David beat the giant bully.

God's people were very proud of David.
He was so brave!
Many years later, he became their king.

Daniel and the Lions

Darius was a mighty king.
He had 120 men to help him rule his kingdom.
One of these men was named Daniel.

Daniel prayed to God every morning,
every lunchtime, and every night.
He was so wise that Darius decided
to make him his *chief* minister.

The other leaders were furious.
"Make a new law," they told the king.
"Everyone must pray to *you* – and to no one else.
Anyone who disobeys will be flung into a pit of lions."

Messengers announced this new law throughout the land. Some men were watching Daniel's house. Sure enough, they saw him pray to God – just the same as before.

They rushed off to Darius.
"We've seen Daniel praying to his God,"
they sneaked.
Darius felt sad because he really admired Daniel.

"Daniel must be thrown to the lions!" said the men.
Soldiers marched Daniel to the lions' pit
and threw him in.

The king couldn't sleep. He kept thinking
of poor Daniel being eaten by the lions.
Next morning, the king rushed to the lions' pit.
"Daniel!" he shouted. "Are you there?"

"I'm here and I'm fine!" said Daniel.
"Not a scratch on me!"
There stood Daniel, safe and sound.

"How come you're not hurt?" asked Darius.
"God sent an angel to shut the lions' mouths,"
said Daniel. "They simply *couldn't* bite me!"

Darius was so happy!
"Pull Daniel out of the lions' pit," he shouted.
"Then go and arrest those men who spied on him."

"From today, everyone must pray to Daniel's God,"
ordered Darius. "He is the living God.
This is the law. It cannot be changed!"

Jonah Gets the Message

"Go to the city of Nineveh!" God told Jonah.
"Tell the people there how bad they are."

But Jonah was scared of doing what God said.
So he ran away instead.
He jumped on a ship and set sail across the sea!

But God sent a great storm.
The ship rocked and rolled and almost sank.
The sailors felt horribly scared!

Jonah hid himself away, down inside the boat.
He knew he had disobeyed God.

The sailors came to find him.
"This storm is all my fault!" said Jonah.
"I didn't want to do what God told me."

"Throw me into the sea!
Then the storm will calm down."

So the sailors flung Jonah into the crashing waves.

The storm stopped immediately –
just as Jonah said it would.

At that moment a massive fish swam up.
It swallowed Jonah whole. *Gulppp!*

"Lord, save me!" he prayed from inside the fish.
"I beg you to help me."

God heard Jonah pray.
Soon the fish spat Jonah out onto the seashore.

This time Jonah did exactly what God said.
"You have done wrong," he told the people of Nineveh.
"Lord God, we are very sorry," they prayed.
They turned their lives around.

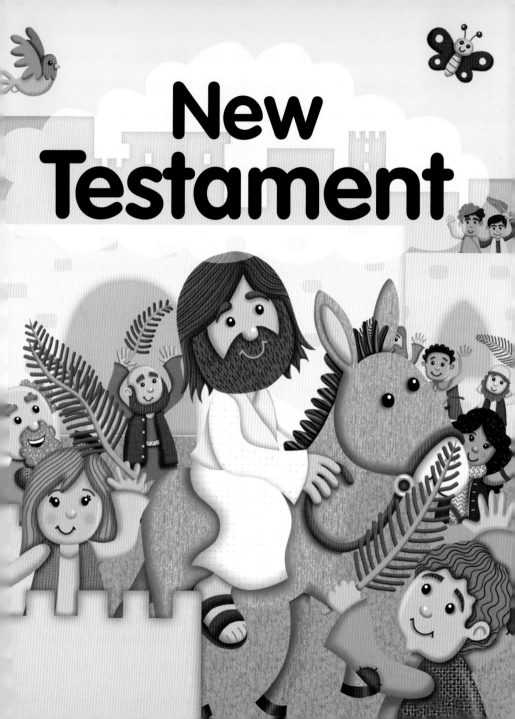

New Testament

Good News for Mary

Mary lived in the town of Nazareth.
One day the angel Gabriel appeared to her.
"Don't be frightened, Mary," said the angel.
"God is going to give you a very special baby!"

Mary was engaged to Joseph the carpenter.
An angel told Joseph about the baby in a dream.
Soon Mary and Joseph got married.
They started to prepare for the baby.

Then one day Joseph read a notice.
"Mary," he said. "It says we have to go to my
home town, Bethlehem, to be counted."
So Mary and Joseph got ready for the journey.

It was a long way and Mary soon felt tired.
"How much further?" she asked Joseph.
At last they saw Bethlehem in the distance.

By the time Mary and Joseph arrived, it was dark.
The town was full of visitors.
"Have you room for us?" asked Joseph at the inn.
"You can sleep in my stable," said the innkeeper.

There, in a borrowed stable, Mary's baby was born.
"We will call him Jesus, as the angel told us," said
Mary. She wrapped her baby in warm cloth.
Joseph laid him to sleep in the animals' manger.

In fields near Bethlehem were some shepherds.
Suddenly an angel appeared to them.
"A baby who will save the world is born
in Bethlehem," the angel told them.

Then a crowd of angels appeared, praising God.
"Let's go and see this baby!" said the shepherds.
They quickly found the stable.
When they saw baby Jesus, they all knelt down.

Old and New Kings

In the East lived some wise men.
"Look – there's a bright, new star!" said one of them.
"That means a great, new king is born," said another.

So the wise men set out to search for this new king.
They followed the star many miles.
At last they came to the great city of Jerusalem.

The wise men went to the palace of King Herod.
"Where is the new king?" they asked.
Herod didn't know, so he called for his advisers.
"This new king is born in Bethlehem," they told him.

So Herod sent the wise men to find the baby king.
They followed the star till it stopped over Bethlehem.
There the wise men found Jesus. They gave him
rich gifts: gold, frankincense, and myrrh.

Jesus Helps a Little Girl

This little girl lived in a town near Lake Galilee.
Her father was named Jairus.

One day she woke up feeling sick.
Doctors came, but the girl still didn't feel better.
Her father, Jairus, grew very worried.

"Have you heard of this healer, Jesus?"
Jairus asked his wife. "He's here in our town."
"Then go and find him!" said his wife.
"Perhaps he can help our little girl."

Jairus hurried to the beach. He found a big crowd there.
"Look, Jesus is in that boat!" said a man.
When the boat reached shore, Jesus climbed out.

"Please come and heal my daughter,"
Jairus asked Jesus. "She's very ill."
"I'll come at once," said Jesus. "Let's go!"

Suddenly a messenger pushed through the crowd.
"Jairus!" he said. "I'm afraid it's too late!
Your little girl has died."

"Don't be afraid!" Jesus comforted Jairus.
He walked on with Jairus, and a crowd followed.
Near Jairus's house, Jesus told them,
"Don't come any further!"

Jesus heard lots of people weeping and wailing.
"Go away!" he told them.
"The girl isn't dead – she's sleeping."
But they just laughed at him.

When they had gone,
Jesus followed Jairus into the girl's room.
"You're too late," sobbed Jairus's wife.

Gently, Jesus took the little girl's hand.
"My dear, get up!" he said.

Jairus's daughter opened her eyes.
Then she sat up and looked around.
Her parents hugged her and wept for joy.

"Fetch your little girl something to eat," said Jesus.
Once she had eaten, she felt much better.
Jesus had done a wonderful miracle:
he healed Jairus's daughter.

The Boy Who Gave Jesus His Lunch

One day a young boy heard Jesus was coming.
His mother packed his lunch: five little loaves
and two fish. Then off he ran to see Jesus.

Jesus had come to the hills for a rest.
But when he saw the crowds of people waiting,
he felt sorry for them.

Sick people came to Jesus.
He put his hands on them – and they were well.
They could see, they could hear, they could walk
and run again! Jesus did many miracles.

After this, Jesus started to tell the people
some of his wonderful stories.
The boy listened carefully.
He didn't want to miss a single word.

The day went on and the sun began to set.
Everyone was now feeling tired and hungry.
They hadn't brought *any* food with them.

"Master!" said Jesus' friends.
"Shall we send these people away to buy food?"
"No – we have to feed them here," answered Jesus.

Jesus' friends went around the crowd.
"Has anyone brought food?" they asked.
Everyone shook their heads.

Suddenly the little boy remembered his lunch.
"I have a little bread," he told one of Jesus' friends.
"And some fish. Jesus can have them all."

"Master," the man said to Jesus,
"Here's a boy with five loaves and two fish."
Jesus smiled and took the food.

"Tell everyone to sit down," Jesus told his friends.
Jesus thanked God for the food.
Then he gave it to his friends.
They took it to the crowds of people.

To the boy's amazement, Jesus went on and on,
giving out bread and fish.
"How can so little become so much?" he thought.
There were more than 5,000 people
– and every one of them had enough to eat.

When they'd finished, Jesus told his friends
to pick up the leftovers.
"Twelve baskets full of scraps," thought the boy.
"And I brought one little basket of food.
This really is a miracle!"

The Searching Shepherd

Jesus told this wonderful story.
There was once a shepherd.
He was a good, kind shepherd.

He had *exactly* one hundred sheep.
Not ninety-seven.
Not one hundred and three.
He had *exactly* one hundred sheep.

The shepherd loved his sheep.
Every day he led them to a grassy meadow.
He guarded them from fierce, prowling wolves.

The shepherd used his crook
to beat off hungry bears.

Each night the shepherd led his flock of sheep safely home to the sheepfold.

Then he counted his sheep.
"One, two, three, four, five… 97, 98, 99, 100."
All his sheep were safe!

One night the shepherd counted his sheep,
just the same as usual.
"One, two, three, four, five…"

"… 97, 98, 99… Oh no!"
He must have missed one sheep.

He started counting all over again.
"One, two, three, four, five…" Still only 99!
One sheep was certainly missing.
The shepherd left the 99 sheep safe in their fold.
Then he set off into the night to find his lost sheep.

The shepherd searched in muddy streams.
Nothing!
He looked in empty barns.
Nothing!
He peered into dark woods…
Nothing!

The shepherd walked for miles and miles.
He grew very hungry.
He grew very, very tired.

"Baa!"
The shepherd stopped still.
He cupped his ear and listened.
It must be his lost sheep!

The shepherd walked towards the sound.
He lifted his lost sheep from the bush
where it had got caught.
Its woollen coat was straggly and torn.

The shepherd lifted his dear, lost sheep
onto his shoulders.
Gently, he carried it home.

He reached the sheep-pen and counted again.
"… 97, 98, 99, 100." All his sheep were safely home.
The shepherd went off to find his friends.
"Come and have a party!" he said.
"I've found my sheep that was lost."

How pleased the shepherd was
that he'd found his lost sheep again.
God is happy too, when Jesus finds lost people
and they return to him.

The Loving Father

There was once a rich farmer.
He had a beautiful house, many servants,
great flocks of sheep, and herds of cows.
Best of all, he had two sons who he loved very much.

One day the younger son went to his father.
"Dad," he said. "You've got lots of money.
Can I have my share now?
Then I can leave home and have a big adventure."

The boy's father felt sorry
that his son wanted to leave home.
But he gave the boy his share of his money.

That very same day, the younger son left home.
His father was very sad.
Each morning he climbed to the roof of his house,
hoping he might see his son returning.

The younger son journeyed for days.
At last he reached a great city.
There he bought himself a huge house.

He had lots of money and made lots of friends.
He gave lots of parties.
His friends came and ate lots of his food.
He was having a grand time!

Then one day all the money ran out.
No more parties!
The younger son's friends all disappeared too.

No work.
No money…
What was he to do?

At last a farmer took pity on the young man.
"I'll pay you to look after my pigs," he said.
So the young man went to work
in the farmer's pigsty.

He fed the pigs and cleaned out the straw.
He was so hungry he even ate the pigs' food!
After a time, he started to feel very sorry for himself.

"The *servants* in Dad's house get better food than this,"
he said to himself one day.
"I'll go home and tell Dad I'll work as his servant."

So the young man set off on the long walk home.

As usual, his father was watching
from the roof of his house.
He saw a tiny figure in the distance.
Could it be his son?

It was!
The father ran to meet his long-lost son.
"Dad, I'm so sorry…" said the young man.
"I don't deserve to be your son any more.
Please let me work as one of your servants!"

But his father just laughed.
"Bring my son my best gold ring and cloak," he said.
That same night the father threw a party.
"Be happy!" he said. "My son, who was lost, is found!"

Jesus said, "God is happy too,
when he welcomes home people who are lost."

The Stranger Who Cared

There was once a man who had
to walk from Jerusalem to Jericho.
He packed his bags and set out early.

But as the day went on, the road got steeper
and the sun grew hotter.
He was worried he wouldn't arrive
in Jericho before night fell.

All at once, there was a shout!
Before the man knew what was happening,
robbers had leapt from behind the rocks.
They stole the man's bags and his clothes.
Then they ran off.

The poor man lay on the road.
His head ached. His body ached.
What was he to do?

Suddenly he heard a *flip-flop, flip-flop* sound.
It was a priest walking to Jerusalem.
Surely he would help!

The man called out, "Help! Help!"
But the priest crossed to the other side of the road
and walked on. *Flip-flop, flip.*
The sound of his sandals died away.

The injured man lay still again.
Suddenly he heard the *clomp-clomp* of boots.
This time it was a worker from the Temple.
The man called out, "Help! Please help me!"

The official looked around in fright.
As soon as he saw the injured man,
he crossed the road and walked faster.
Straight past the poor man.

No one else came along the road.
The sun was sinking in the sky. The man lay still.
Suddenly he heard a faint *clip-clop, clip-clop.*
It was a donkey!

The man saw it was a stranger from another country.
He certainly wouldn't help!
But when the stranger reached the man, he stopped.
He walked over to the injured man.

"What's happened here?" he asked kindly.
"You look in a bad way."
"Thieves stole everything I had," explained the man.
"They beat me up and left me lying in the road!"

The stranger went back to his donkey.
He brought out bandages and oil
and bathed the man's wounds.

The stranger lifted the hurt man
onto the donkey's back.
By now it was getting dark,
and the stars were coming out.

They set off down the road,
slowly and carefully.

At last they reached a house.
The stranger lifted the injured man down.

"Look after my friend," the stranger said.
"Here's some money.
Please make sure my friend has plenty to eat
and all the right medicine."

Jesus told this story about a stranger who helped. He said we should help *anyone* who needs us – not just our friends.

A Farmer Sows Seeds

There was once a farmer
who went to sow seeds in his field.
He walked up and down,
scattering handfuls of seeds as he went.

Some of his seeds fell on the path.
Here the soil was packed hard.

Many people walked along the path.
They trampled on the seeds.

Flocks of birds swooped down
and gobbled up seeds
they found lying on the path.

Some seeds fell on rocks.
Here the soil was thin and dry.

Seeds that fell on the rocks soon sprouted.
But the roots couldn't find any water.
When the sun shone, these plants withered away.

Some of the seeds fell among weeds and thorns.
These seeds started to grow.

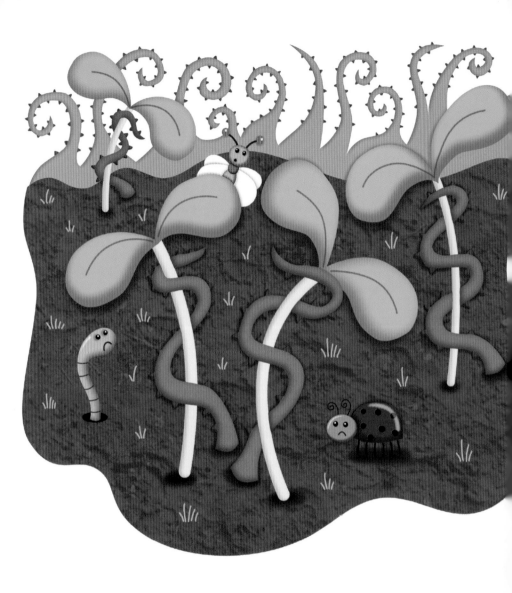

But the thorns soon choked the farmer's plants.

Yet some of the farmer's seeds fell on good soil.
These seeds sprouted.

The seeds that fell on good soil
grew into full ears of grain.
There were a hundred times more
than the farmer had sowed.

Jesus explained this story to his friends.
"Sowing the seeds is like sowing God's message,"
Jesus said.

"Some falls on the path, or on rocky ground.

"People get excited by God's message
– but soon they give up.

"But some falls on good soil.
People hear God's message,
and keep it in their heart."

Two Builders – Two Houses

Once two men each decided to build a house.

The first man was in a great rush and a hurry.

He quickly found some sandy ground.
"What a great place for my house!" he thought.
"The sooner I finish, the sooner I can have a rest!"

He was in such a hurry he didn't
bother digging foundations for his house.
He found stones nearby for the walls.

He used logs to hold up the roof.
In no time at all his house was finished.

But the second man had hardly started.
He searched carefully for the best place for his house.
Finally he found a high, rocky place.
"This will be great for building a house!" he thought.

The second man wanted to do a really good job.
He dug very deep foundations for his new house.

The second man was busy from morning till night.
He chose the biggest stones and the strongest logs.
At last his house was finished too.

Almost at once dark clouds gathered.
Rain began to fall.
The little stream grew into a great river.

Lightning flashed!
Thunder roared!
The first man watched in alarm.

CRRRAASHH!!!
The roof of his house fell in.
SWOOOOSSH!!!
His house fell completely flat!
The foolish man, who built his house on sand,
was left with – nothing!

The second man ran inside his home.
He had built on rock.
The second man's house stood firm in the storm.

Jesus said, "People who listen to my words
and put them into action
are like the wise man,
who built his house on rock."

Jesus the King

There was an important festival in Jerusalem.
Jesus went with his special friends,
the twelve disciples.

Jesus borrowed a donkey and rode into Jerusalem. The crowds got very excited. They shouted *"Hosanna!"* and waved palm tree branches.

On the day of the festival,
Jesus ate a special supper with his disciples
in an upstairs room.

Jesus broke bread and poured wine
and gave them to his disciples.
But one disciple, Judas, was plotting against Jesus.
He slipped out.

After supper, Jesus took his disciples to a garden.
"Stay here and pray," he said.
Jesus prayed too.

Suddenly a crowd of soldiers appeared,
led by Judas. They took Jesus away.

They stood Jesus before the ruler, Pilate.
"I find *nothing* wrong with him," said Pilate.
"Jesus is making trouble," people shouted.
"He *must* be killed!" So Pilate sent Jesus to die.

Soldiers put Jesus on a wooden cross.
At midday, the sky went dark.
Jesus cried out. Then he died.
Jesus' family and friends watched sadly.

A good man named Joseph took Jesus' body.
Gently, he put it in a rock tomb.
Then he rolled a huge stone across the doorway.

Jesus Lives!

Early Sunday morning, women went to the tomb.
The stone was rolled away, but they couldn't see
Jesus' body. Two shining men stood there.
"Jesus isn't here!" said one. "He is risen from the dead."

The women rushed back to tell the disciples.
At first they didn't believe the women.
But then Jesus appeared to them too.

A few weeks later,
Jesus climbed a hill with his disciples.
As they watched,
he was taken up into heaven.

And now Jesus lives forever!